STOP PROCRASTINATING

Simple Steps to Increase Productivity and Overcome Procrastination

Robert Hensley

CONTENTS

Introduction 7

Chapter 1 Science behind Procrastination 9

What is procrastination 9

   The psychological phenomenon of procrastination 10

Why we procrastinate: Causes of procrastination .. 10

   Tossing self-compassion to the wind 11

   Learning procrastination from role models 11

   Thinking that you will not be effective in the task 12

   Bias over certain tasks 12

   Estimation of time is a little off 12

   Focusing less on future gains and more on present gains 13

   Being too much of a perfectionist 13

   Anxiety and depression 14

   Having discomfort intolerance 14

   The Procrastination-Action Line 15

Chapter 2 What People Don't Tell You about Procrastination 17

   Procrastination is not about time management 17

   Procrastination losses you precious time 18

   Procrastination Blows opportunities 18

   Procrastination will not allow you to meet your goals 19

   Procrastination ruins people's careers 19

   Procrastination risks lowering your self-esteem 20

   Procrastination allows poor decision-making 20

Procrastination damages reputations 21
Procrastination puts your health at risk 21

Chapter 3 Steps on How to Stop Procrastinating 22

Step 1: Identify your triggers 22

Perfectionist 22

Ostrich 23

Self-saboteur 23

Daredevil 23

Chicken 24

Step 2: Start facing your triggers and get rid of them 24

Perfectionist 24

Ostriches 25

Self-saboteurs 25

Daredevils 25

Chicken 26

Step 3: Take planned breaks 26

Step 4: Reward yourself 27

Step 5: Make the consequences of procrastination immediate 28

Step 6: Ensure that you keep track of your time 28

Step 7: Design your future actions 29

Step 8: Make all your tasks more achievable 29

Chapter 4 Actionable Tips to Help You Overcome Procrastination 31

Break your work into short steps 31

Prioritize tasks 32

The Ivy Lee method 32
The Eisenhower Matrix 32
Determine your productivity cycle 33
Set deadlines for yourself 33
  Are the deadlines concrete? 34
  Are your deadlines realistic? 34
  Are your deadlines meaningful? 34
Use timeboxing 35
Have a to-do list 36
Establish streaks 36
Gamify your habits 36
Establish a routine 37
Commit to having no "zero days" 37
Plan well for future contingencies 37
Increase your energy levels 38
  Getting sufficient sleep 38
  Drink enough water 38
  Eat a healthy meal 38
  Exercise 39
Get rid of distractions 39
Get rid of bottlenecks 40
Just getting it done 40
Modify it 40
Delegate it 40
Eliminate it completely 41
Avoid a perfectionist mindset 41

Visualize your future self 42

Identify someone to hold you accountable 42

Seek favorable peer influence 43

Chapter 5 Strategies that Can Help You Change 44

Stage 1: Pre-contemplation 44

Stage 2: Contemplation 45

Stage 3: Preparation 46

Stage 4: Action 46

Stage 5: Maintenance 46

Stage 6: Termination 47

Experiment and Reassess 48

Start your day on fire 48

Vocalizing 48

Practicing daily 49

First things first 49

Chapter 6 The Power of Nice 51

The role of self-criticism in procrastination 51

The role of self-compassion in procrastination 52

Learn to forgive yourself 53

Chapter 7 The Art of Emotion Surfing 55

Learn to surf your emotions 55

Start from the basics 56

Get your feet wet 56

Understand the weather 57

Make friends with the waves 58

Harness the power of the emotion 58

Surf your emotions like a guru 58

Chapter 8 Establish a Strong Willpower 60

Do not keep yourself in a constant state of depleted willpower 61

Use your imagination 62

Think of something else 63

Build good habits because you will need them when you are down 63

Take one step at a time 64

Be yourself 65

Do not expose yourself to temptations, and if you do, have a plan 65

Chapter 9 Simplify Your Life 67

Practical ways to simplify your life 69

Spend at least 10 minutes meditating 69

Work on your posture 69

Keep a food diary 70

Use your opposite hand 70

Correct your speech 71

Create and then meet self-imposed deadlines 71

Keep track of your spending 72

Be mindful of your automatic decisions 72

One Last Word 74

OTHER BOOKS BY ROBERT HENSLEY

Productivity Habits: Proven Techniques to Increase Personal Productivity and Achieve Goals (Time management and Productivity Series Book 1)

Introduction

Tick tock, tick-tock, the sound of the clock! "It's Friday noon, and I need to submit the monthly report before 6 p.m." You find yourself working furiously to beat the deadline and still have the work done to standard. Inside, you are silently cursing yourself for not starting the report early enough; after all, you had 30 days to work on it!

How did I end up here? What am I going to do? What made me lose my focus?

The answer is simple- procrastination! You knew right from the beginning of the month that you had to work on the report, but you shoved it aside and told yourself you would work on it tomorrow, after all, I still have 29 days, then 25, 14, 5 and eventually the deadline is a few hours away! You spent so much time re-reading your emails, chatting with friends on WhatsApp, rumor mongering on social media, taking unnecessarily long coffee breaks, and tasks that did not need your immediate attention.

Does that sound familiar? Well, trust me, you are not alone!

One thing that we all have to understand is that procrastination is a vortex that has trapped many people. Research shows that over 95% of the world's population procrastinates to some extent in life. In spite the fact that it is comforting to know that you are not the only victim of procrastination, one thing that you have to realize is that it is the reason why you are still behind and are not reaching your full potential.

What is interesting is that so many people think that procrastination is laziness. Well, these two are quite distinct from each other. It does not matter how organized you are and how committed you are to your work. There is a high chance that you have found yourself wasting away hours on trivial stuff like shopping online, updating your Facebook status, and what have you. The time that you should spend on work-related projects.

It is important to note that procrastination is such an active process in which you choose to pursue something different from tasks you know very well that you should be performing. So procrastination is not laziness! Laziness is simply inactivity and lack of willingness to act. On the other hand, procrastination is you choosing an enjoyable task that is not urgent and ignoring a task that you deem unpleasant but likely to be very urgent and important.

However, what you have to realize is that when you give in to this impulse, there is serious consequences that will accompany it — for instance, guilt and shame. Think about what procrastination will do to your productivity at work, your goals, and even your reputation? Trust me, it is not a good thing, and am glad we both agree on this one.

The good news is that this book aims at helping us identify reasons why we procrastinate and practical ways on how we can overcome them so that we can take back control over our life. Come with me and let's get started!

Chapter 1 Science behind Procrastination

What is procrastination

Procrastination is a term that has been there for centuries. It indicates that the problem is something that goes way back. Socrates and Aristotle, the ancient Greek Philosophers, used the word Akrasia to describe the habit of procrastination. Akrasia means acting against your judgment. In other words, you chose to do something even when you know that you should be spending that time doing something else.

To define procrastination, you can say that it is delaying a task or a set of tasks to some other time. Therefore, you can use the term Akrasia or procrastination, and they all refer to that force that prevents you from following through on what you are supposed to be doing in the first place.

For instance, if you are supposed to write a report for your company's annual review, you keep postponing it, and instead, you spend so much of that time surfing the internet, Chatting with friends or shopping online among other things.

The problem with this is that this often stands in the way of you pursuing goals that matter. In such a case, you may tarnish your reputation at work or even end up getting fired. Other negative impacts of procrastination include; high levels of stress, anxiety, and depression, among other mental health issues.

The psychological phenomenon of procrastination

Procrastination is a phenomenon that lies in the heart of the psychological understanding of goal attainment. One thing that you have to understand is that, for you to attain your goals, you have to be motivated and capable of performing all necessary tasks that satisfy the goal. Particularly, procrastination is a subject that is relevant to industrialized cultures that emphasize adherence to schedules.

Even though so many researchers argue that procrastination is a modern phenomenon, so many concepts similar to this have been in existence for ages. The ancient Egyptians also used words that related to procrastination. Procrastination was used in the 17th century, as indicated in the Oxford dictionary. During this time, it was used to describe certain situations in which people chose to restrain from their habits with intelligence just so that they could arrive at better inferences. It was not until the 18th century that the negative consequences of procrastination were discussed.

Why we procrastinate: Causes of procrastination

It is one of the most important questions when it comes to addressing the negative impact that procrastination has on our lives and attainment of our goals. According to statistics, it is estimated that at least $1/5^{th}$ of adults in the world procrastinate. Also, 50% of students in the world are victims of procrastination.

One longitudinal study indicates that procrastination is a self-defeating habit that has short term benefits, but in the long term, the impact is detrimental. Which begs the question, why do we procrastinate? While further research will help in unpacking the complexity of this behavioral pattern, we all agree that each person has a unique reason for procrastinating tasks. The only cure to this is for us to respond to the reasons specific to you as an individual.

Here are some of the common causes of procrastination:

Tossing self-compassion to the wind

According to one journal on Self-Identity, researchers reported that people with less self-compassion were highly likely to be more stressed when performing tasks. In effect, increases their chances of postponing them to other times.

To overcome this, it is important that you understand the impact that this has on your personality and your reputation. Take time to have some serious self-talk with yourself while ensuring that you exercise kindness. One of the things that you have to come to terms with is that you are human and maintain optimism in everything instead of going down the road of negative criticism.

Learning procrastination from role models

Well, so many people procrastinate because that is what they have seen their role models do time and time again. It can be your parents, friend, or siblings, among others. If the person that you admire most is a victim of procrastination, the chances are that you will ape their behavior by putting off important tasks.

It is critical that you spend some time talking to yourself on the negative impact that these role models might have faced as a result of their procrastination. Then ensure that you review all other options for new role models who are always willing to act and reap positive outcomes because of it.

Thinking that you will not be effective in the task

Sometimes, the reason you procrastinate is that you think that you are not skilled enough or well cut out for the task at hand. If you feel that your skills are inadequate, get an upgrade by taking several causes or having someone to teach you the ropes. If you need guidance and help from an expert, go for it.

Sometimes, you will realize that you have the skills but are afraid to fail. One thing that you have to understand is that the primary element of success lies in your mindset. Rather than allowing negative self-talk and thoughts convince you otherwise, begin to turn those thoughts into positive ones. Use positive affirmations like "I can do it; I am qualified to do this" among others.

No one is perfect. However, you have to be willing to give yourself a chance to try and learn as you go. You have to step out of your comfort zone so that you can tap into your growth mindset. You will be surprised just how smart and equipped you are!

Bias over certain tasks

The other reason may be that there are certain tasks you like doing while there are those that you feel unmotivated about. It explains the reason why you find yourself saying, "I can do most things, but not this one."

Well, the truth is, you can do it, you just have bias over what you find enjoyable and what is not. The best thing you can do is to challenge yourself to do it. Have an open mind and prove your bias wrong. It is essential that you use that opportunity to prove that voice within you wrong and work towards combating that bias once and for all.

Estimation of time is a little off

Sometimes, when you are given a task or assignment to do, you may estimate that you will take five days to complete it. However, you fail to put into perspective all the details of the task and how that will impact on time. This is what is often referred to as planning fallacy.

Rather than just putting time on a task, it is important that you make it a habit to start each task as soon as you get it so that you have adequate time to solve every problem and seek clarifications where necessary. This will help compensate for time deficiencies. Once you complete the task successfully, reward yourself. It not only motivates you to make it a culture completing tasks beforehand, but also helps you become a better planner.

Focusing less on future gains and more on present gains

This is what is referred to as short-range hedonism in rational emotive behavior therapy (REBT). When you chose to focus on your present and all the tasks therein, there is a high likelihood that you develop low frustration tolerance. In other words, when tougher situations and tasks face you, the chances are that you will not be able to endure.

It is critical that you remind yourself to always look at the bigger picture in every situation. This will help you bring into perspective all the future gains you stand to enjoy hence deemphasizing on present frustrations.

Being too much of a perfectionist

One thing that you need to bear in mind is that you are not perfect, and so is anything you do. When you look at a task at hand and think that it has to be perfect, then you each time you start to work on it, you feel that it does not meet your "set high standards." This, in turn, keeps you from making any progress at all.

Therefore, it is critical that you diminish the importance of performing tasks with perfection in mind. Instead, emphasize on giving each task the importance and urgency it deserves. This way, you will perform each task to your level best and complete it promptly. To make this more effective, create two lists: one of the examples of tasks when perfectionism has been helpful; and another when timely completion has been helpful.

Anxiety and depression

If there is anything I have learned over the years is that when you are overly anxious or depressed, the chances are that your concentration, motivation, and perseverance will be significantly diminished. It means that your performance is affected and completion of tasks will not be completed within the agreed upon time.

If you are depressed, the very first thing that you should do is seek medical attention or seek the help of a professional therapist. It will go a long way in helping to rule out any physical causes to your anxiety so that you can get the proper treatment you need to stay focused and achieving your goals. You will also learn tricks on how to break your tasks into smaller micro-goals that you can complete and eventually contribute to the attainment of the bigger task/goal.

Having discomfort intolerance

This often is the reason why you are disengaged from the task(s) at hand. According to REBT, procrastination is thought to arise from a belief that one should always avoid discomfort. It means that each time you feel that you are uncomfortable both physically and mentally, you simply practice procrastination.

Well, the truth is, if you keep doing this, the chances are that you will stagnate in life and miss your window of opportunity and let success slide. The trick is for you to challenge yourself withstand as much discomfort as possible, starting from less discomfort and gradually progressing to the end.

Additionally, always see it as a chance to encourage yourself to engage in various tasks even if it is only for a short while. Pay attention to the long-term reward that awaits you once you have persevered. If you stick with that in mind, you will realize that discomfort will slowly contribute to your growth and change your mindset to have the "I can do" mentality.

The Procrastination-Action Line

One important thing that you have to notice is that you cannot depend on long-term consequences and rewards to stay motivated. In other words, it is important for you to find a way to visualize future rewards in the present time. It simply means that you have to be willing to make future rewards and punishments applicable in the present time.

Let us consider the report writing for your Company's annual review we just highlighted earlier. The truth is, you have known about the report for a couple of weeks, but you chose to put it off. You must have felt a rush of adrenaline (pain) each time you thought about the report and the fact that you have not done it yet, but then you chose to do nothing about it. Suddenly, the deadline date is here, and the future consequences can now be felt in the present. What you did was you allowed procrastination to escalate to the point where it crossed the "Action line."

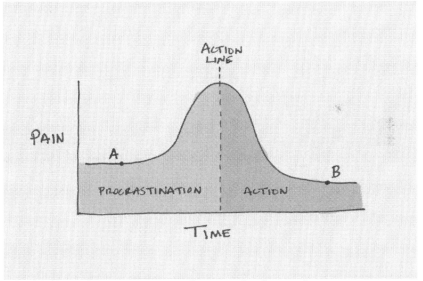

It is important to understand that, the moment you crossed the action line, pain begins to reduce. When you are in the middle of procrastinating, the pain is high as compared to when you are in the middle of work.

In the above graph, it is evident that Point A is much more painful than when you are at point B. In other words, when you keep postponing tasks, the chances are that you will experience heightened levels of shame, anxiety, and shame. What is even more interesting is the fact that these emotions are much higher than the effort that would have otherwise been spent getting work done.

Note that, the problem is not getting the work done; it is starting the work in the first place. If you want to stop postponing things, it is critical that you make it easy for yourself to trust that once you get started, motivation and momentum will follow suit.

Chapter 2 What People Don't Tell You about Procrastination

There are so many things that people do not tell you about procrastination. However, these things are very important to take note of if you are going to make the most of your energy and seize every opportunity life has to offer. Some of these things include;

Procrastination is not about time management

It is important to note that procrastination is not an issue of time management. Most of the people I know who suffer from procrastination often are good at managing their time. Well, they sometimes are too optimistic about their allocation of time, but that is not the reason behind their postponing.

Let us consider an example; when I got my first job, I had everything figured out (at least I thought so); get up very early in the morning, meditate, work out, hit the shower, eat the day's frog and the list goes on. Trust me; everything was well laid out to seconds!

You would not imagine what happened; every time my

alarm went on; I hit the snooze button and ended up getting up at 8 am with all the guilt and shame just to hit the shower and get to work at 9 am. The truth is I could not manage to follow through with my plan. This was not a time management issue; it was more of a self-discipline issue. I lacked important emotional regulation skills or self-discipline to rise above the negative emotion associated with certain tasks.

Therefore, you have to realize that, if you are going to beat procrastination, then you have to be able to manage your feelings, thoughts, and actions and not managing time. So, whatever your reason for procrastination, there are so many negative effects that this has on your life and may damage your future. Here are some of the effects that people might not tell you about;

Procrastination losses you precious time

Have you ever stopped to take count of the amount of time you have lost procrastinating? Well, it may not be easy to count it down to microseconds, but you can reflect and tell that it is much time.

The worst thing that often happens is that five or ten years down the line, you wake up and wonder where all that time went because you are the same as you were five years or ten years ago. You do not want to experience that feeling! No one can turn back the hands of time. You have to suck it up and live with your regret. Is this how you want to live your life? Is this how you want to wake up ten years from today? Most certainly not. Therefore, realize that time is the most precious gift you have and you had better start making the most of it get what you desire.

Procrastination Blows opportunities

God knows we had wasted so many opportunities because we failed to leverage them when they are presented to us. Sometimes, you let those opportunities slide because you think that you are busy doing something else or that you will express interest later, and before you know it, the doors have closed. That is when you want to kick yourself hard.

The thing that you fail to realize is that maybe that could have changed your life for the better. The sad news is that such good opportunities are only coming knocking at your door once and so you do not have a second chance at them. Realize that opportunities are a way in which the world is offering you more. Therefore, please do yourself a favor and seize them without hesitation.

Procrastination will not allow you to meet your goals

One interesting thing about procrastination is the fact that it tends to come with full force whenever you think of some goals you would like to achieve or when you desire to make changes in your life. The truth is, sometimes you want something, but you seem not to have the courage to take the very first step.

Well, this can be very confusing, and you even find yourself wondering why it is so hard to go for something that you strongly desire. The only person that can answer this question is you. It is critical that you start by exploring that internal resistance within you. You have to think about ways you can shake off that procrastination so that you can take advantage of the possibilities before you for a better life. Realize that, if you keep postponing, the chances are that you will not realize your goals.

Procrastination ruins people's careers

One thing that you have to understand is that how you perform affects your results directly. It affects how much you achieve and if you work at an organization that requires you to meet targets, this might well be affected too. However, the most important question you should ask yourself is what impact this will have on your career eventually.

The truth is I have seen people who have lost their jobs, missed promotions, or tarnished their reputation at work. Yes, you will try hard to hide it at first, but this will eventually come out and crush your career. Therefore, ensure that you are not undermining your performance unnecessarily.

Procrastination risks lowering your self-esteem

This is a vicious cycle that you are likely to find yourself. The reason why some people procrastinate is that they have low self-esteem. However, what is more, is that procrastination worsens it by lowering it further. It is when you start asking yourself what could be wrong and why you cannot seem to stop it.

One thing that you have to realize is that having low self-esteem often risks holding you back from pursuing what matters most, and you end up engaging in actions that are self-destructing. In other words, it is through procrastination that your confidence is chipped away little by little.

If this is something that you have found yourself in, the first thing to do is start working on rebuilding your self-esteem. Let go of the illusion that you should be doing something. The danger in this is that you will force yourself into things when you are not ready. Work on your mindset and replace every negative thought with positive ones.

Procrastination allows poor decision-making

Realize that when you keep postponing activities and tasks, there is a high chance that you will make decisions from that standpoint. The chances are that these decisions are poor because of the circumstances at hand. In other words, you will be making decisions because of the pressure that you are running out of time. You are simply looking for a quick-fix even when it is not the best option.

Understand that emotions influence what decisions we make, and when we procrastinate, our feelings are affected to a larger extent. This impacts our happiness, outcomes, and life in general.

Procrastination damages reputations

When you keep procrastinating things, there is a high chance that you lose the trust of the people around you, and that eats away your reputation. You have to realize that no one wants to hold on to someone who gives empty promises.

Other than damaging your reputation, your confidence and sense of self-worth are utterly affected. With time, you realize that it gets easier to postpone things because it is no longer a surprise to you or anyone around you. Gradually, your clients begin to pull away, and you no longer get offers and opportunities coming your way. Trust me; this is not what you want.

Procrastination puts your health at risk

Research studies have shown that procrastination is linked to mental health problems. These include anxiety and depression. If by procrastinating, you become depressed, this may affect your productivity over time. The truth is, when you keep postponing things you are supposed to address immediately, there is a chance that this will stir up anxiety and stress, and this kills you silently from the inside.

On the other hand, if you are procrastinating your check-ups and doctor's appointments, you risk worsening your health situation, and the consequences may be more serious than if you had addressed them sooner. You have to remember that procrastination is a habit, and if you do not break it sooner, it will break you!

Chapter 3 Steps on How to Stop Procrastinating

There are quite several steps you can follow to stop procrastination. Some of these steps include:

Step 1: Identify your triggers

This is the very first step to overcoming procrastination. You cannot stop something if you do not know what it is you are stopping in the first place. The only way you are going to stop procrastinating is by knowing what kind of procrastinator you are. Here are some of the procrastinator types and what triggers each type has.

Perfectionist

Well, every perfectionist takes pleasure in always being perfect in what they do. Even though perfection means doing the work impeccably down to the details, you have to realize that while you are in pursuit of perfection, you risk getting cold feet to do the work. The reason being, you may be scared to show imperfections while at it.

Because of this, there is a high likelihood that you fail to bring projects to completion as required. Mainly because you are waiting for the perfect time, the perfect approach, the perfect team, among others. In other words, you allow your desire for perfection to get in the way of your work, and you get trapped in a vicious cycle of additions, deletions, and edits.

Ostrich

This is someone that often prefers staying in the dreaming phase. This means that they keep postponing work just so that they do not work or deal with the negative impact of work stress. It is through dreaming that such procrastinators get a sense of false achievement. In their minds, they always envision big and overly ambitious plans that they do not get to start working towards them. In other words, all their dreams and plans remain just as they are - Dreams!

Self-saboteur

These are the kind of procrastinators who often believe that by not doing anything, they are safe from bad things happening. In other words, this kind of people often has a strong fear of making mistakes or doing things the wrong way. Therefore, they choose to sit back and do nothing about it just so that they avoid such mishaps. Eventually, they make few mistakes, but not forgetting the fact that they also do not accomplish much.

Daredevil

This is another type of procrastinator who believes that deadlines push them to perform better. In other words, they prefer engaging in activities that please them before the deadline date comes. They like to think that they work best under pressure.

It often comes to them as an unconscious thing. All they think is that if they started doing the work soon as they get it, they are sacrificing all the time they would otherwise be spending doing things that are enjoyable and pleasurable to them. This is often a belief that grows in them based on the number of times they have spent in the past, burning the midnight oil. However, what they fail to realize is that they end up sacrificing the quality of their work because of having to rush through it all to beat the deadlines.

Chicken

This kind of people cannot prioritize their work. In other words, they often do what they feel like doing instead of thinking through all the tasks at hand and then prioritizing them based on the urgency of each task.

It is interesting to note that, such people tend to feel that since prioritizing takes a bit of extra time from their schedules, it is not worth it. Because of that, they end up engaging in tasks that are effortless and do not contribute to the end goals of the project in any way. They spend too much of their time buried in low-impact projects and oblivious on high-priority tasks.

Step 2: Start facing your triggers and get rid of them

Whether your trigger is a fear of failure, avoidance, overwhelming emotions or even trying to convince yourself that you are too busy on other things to get this one done, the truth is that you can work towards improving your abilities so that you not only eliminate these procrastination triggers but also improve your productivity.

Perfectionist

If you are a perfectionist, it is high time you reclarify your goals. Most of the time, you will notice that you are procrastinating because those goals do not make your heart beat anymore. There is no more spark in them and have outgrown them.

Realize that, you are an evolving human being, and so are your goals and dreams. This means that you have to look over your goals and ask yourself whether they are the things that you still want to achieve.

It is critical that you take the time you need to regroup and make a new list of all the things that you would like to achieve. Ask yourself what steps you would like to follow, do the things you are currently engaging in the mirror your dreams, and are there things that need a change in your life to accomplish your heart's desires? Write all these things down on a piece of paper and pin them where you will see every morning you get up to remind you of where you are going!

Ostriches

For ostriches, the first thing that you should do is learn to take on difficult tasks first. Even though you may not be a morning person, you have to accept that this is the time when your brain is most active and productive than other times of the day. Therefore, utilize this time to engage in quite hectic projects.

Understand that if you leave these tasks to other times of the day when you are exhausted or lack the motivation, the chances are that you will put them off or you will deliver average quality. When you complete lots of simple tasks in the morning, you get a false sense of productivity when, in fact, all you have done is read emails and attend meetings!

Self-saboteurs

For you, it is important that you work on writing down a to-do list as well as a not-to-do list at the beginning of each day. Research studies have shown that when you write down things, it is very powerful at improving your abilities psychologically and hence have the zeal to get things done.

Therefore, ensure that you make it a habit to create a list of tasks you aim at working on throughout the day and another of all the things you should avoid. When you do this, all the difficult tasks are drawn to your mind's focus rather than having them locked away in avoidance mode. Once you accomplish tasks, cross them one at a time on the list. Trust, it is so satisfying to check them off your list and offers you more motivation to work on what is still pending.

Daredevils

If you are a daredevil, the first thing that you have to work on is creating a timeline with deadlines. Well, it is quite common to have deadlines for a goal, and this might seem to you as a good idea. However, this is just an open invitation to postponing. It is simply a deadline that you created with no pressure attached to it. This means that each day, something comes up, and you push it back and feel as though you have not done enough to accomplish them.

The secret to overcoming these problems is creating a bigger timeline, and then within it, establish deadlines as you go. The beauty of doing this is that once each deadline is checked off, you set the next one for the next task in line. This way, you remain on track, and you are upbeat and accountable for aligning with the overall bigger timeline.

Chicken

For chickens, it is important that you break tasks into smaller chunks that you can easily bite. Most of the time, the reason why you procrastinate is that what you have on your plate is overwhelming. It feels as though everything is too much for you, and you may not be able to handle it. That way, you get confused, not knowing where to begin. It also applies to instances where you have set yourself vague goals that are not clear and lack proper directions.

The trick here is to break those goals into smaller tasks or micro-goals that you can perform daily or weekly basis. When you have smaller tasks or steps to follow, everything becomes easier and enjoyable. It may appear as a slower approach to achieving the goals, but eventually, when they all come together, you will have met your big goal as fast as possible because of the powerful momentum that micro-goals have.

Step 3: Take planned breaks

One mistake that people often make is working continuously and risks getting tired and having a burnout. It is important to note that the human brain gets tired and need to rest from time to time. One reason why you may be procrastinating may be because you are working continuously without allowing yourself time to rest.

The trick here is to ensure that you have regular and well-structured breaks in between tasks so that when you get back to work, you are refreshed, and energetic to take on activities with enthusiasm and hence, boost your productivity levels.

Taking a short break of even five minutes is quite sufficient to renew your mind, keep it sharp and focused while warding off fatigue. You can download the Pomodoro time tracker to your mobile phone and use it to help you set breaks at intervals. With this online timer, you can start a 5, 15, or 25-minute timer depending on how much you feel is sufficient for you, and then follow the prompts after that.

Step 4: Reward yourself

When you achieve a goal, however small it may be, it is important that you appreciate yourself for that. The best way to do that is to have a reward system for each task. This goes a long way in boosting your sense of motivation, and each time you accomplish something, you trigger the release of feel-good hormones which comes bursting and lifts your spirits and mood spurring you to achieve more.

It is important that each reward you get is proportional to the task accomplished. For instance, a micro-goal can get you your favorite coffee and snack at a special place. If the task was bigger/harder, you could choose to treat yourself to a spa-massage, weekend getaway, among others.

You can also use such apps as Forest to help you stay focused. This app helps turn productivity into a fun game in which you can plant virtual trees at the start of your time. If you keep that focus for the duration the timer runs, you grow as many trees in your forest as much as possible. What is very much fulfilling is working hard to ensure that at the end of the game or by the time the timer goes off, you will have grown a forest.

You can also make the rewards more immediate to make it easy to avoid procrastination. The best approach is to bring all future rewards into the present moment using temptation bundling strategy. This is a concept that came from behavioral economics research, and it suggests that you bundle a good habit in the long-term with a good one in the short-term.

For instance, you can listen to good audiobooks while working out, get a pedicure while processing work emails, or watch your favorite show while folding clothes, among others.

Step 5: Make the consequences of procrastination immediate

Just like you have made the rewards of achieving a task immediately, it is also important that you make the consequences of procrastination immediate. There are so many ways in which you can punish yourself for procrastinating. For instance; if you are working out alone, by skipping your workout time the next time will not impact much on your life. It will not make your health or weight deteriorate immediately. However, if you have been working out with a friend, then skipping the workout makes you look like a jerk. In other words, the results of skipping that workout are felt immediately.

Another strategy you can employ in this case is using services like Stickk to make bets. This means that, if you fail to accomplish the task you were supposed to within the right time, then you give money to a charity you hate. In other words, you are putting more skin in the game while creating consequences that are rather immediate if your tasks are not done the right way and within the right time.

Step 6: Ensure that you keep track of your time

If you want to get rid of the bad habit of procrastination, keep track of how you spend your time each day. When you have clarity of where your time goes, the truth is, you will be more focused on ensuring that you review how productive you have been and areas that need improvement.

Yes, it may not be easy to keep track of your time down to every minute of the day, but with an app like Rescue time, that can be possible. It helps you classify how you spend your time and helps you find out how much time each task takes.

You also choose to label every activity as either productive or non-productive. This way, you can always ensure that you block any possible distractions as much as you can.

Step 7: Design your future actions

Did you know that there is a tool that psychologists use to overcome procrastination? Well, this tool is referred to as a commitment device. This tool plays a very significant role in helping you stop procrastination by simply designing what your future actions will be even before you can get there.

For instance, you can curb your eating habits by simply buying foods in packages rather than having them in one huge pack. You can also stop wasting too much of your time on your phone by getting rid of social media apps you have installed.

In the same way, you can lower your chances of spending too much time watching mindless channel surfing by simply hiding your TV in a closet and having it out when it matters most. If you are addicted to gambling, you can ask that you be added to the banned list of online gambling sites as well as local casinos to ensure that you do not engage in gambling in the future. You can also build an emergency fund by simply having the bank create automatic fund transfers to your savings account. All these are small commitment devices that will help you stop procrastination.

Step 8: Make all your tasks more achievable

As already discussed, the friction that procrastination creates is centered around developing a new habit. Once you get started, the truth is that the pain involved reduces and this helps motivate you to keep working. This goes a long way in helping you visualize your habits as small and easy to get rid of and hence lowering the likelihood of your procrastinating.

To make these habits quite easy to overcome, employ the use of *the 2-minute rule*. This rule states that when you start a new habit, it will take less than two minutes actually to do it. The idea underlying this is to ensure that it is as easy as possible to start and trust that the push is sufficient to carry you through the task once you get started.

It is important to note that, once you get started on a certain task, it is easier to keep doing it as opposed to when you have not started at all. It is the use of the 2-minute rule that procrastination becomes something of the past, making you proactive and ready to act when needed too.

The importance of making tasks more achievable includes:

• When you take small measures of progress, you ensure that the momentum is maintained over a long period meaning that there is a high likelihood of completing the tasks.

• The sooner you finish a task, the more quickly you develop new habits, attitudes or productivity and working efficiently.

Chapter 4 Actionable Tips to Help You Overcome Procrastination

Break your work into short steps

One of the reasons why you find yourself procrastinating is because you find the work overwhelming in your subconscious. The best thing that you can do is break a big goal into small micro-goals. Then break each micro-goal on smaller steps or tasks that you can follow to accomplish them. Once you have done that, focus on completing one at a time.

However, if you find yourself still procrastinating even after breaking them into smaller steps, break them further. So, you will realize how simple each task is, and eventually, all the small steps that you now find enjoyable doing contribute to the larger goals. You will wonder why you did not do this sooner.

Let us take an example of a book project that you are working with. The first thing is to break down the whole project into smaller parts that will make it easy to focus and accomplish. You can break it into phases like: research, deciding the topic, creating an outline, drafting the content, creating chapters and writing one chapter at a time, revisions, and creating a cover design, among others.

When you do this, you will realize how simple and manageable the project becomes. What you can do then is to focus on each phase and getting it done to the best of your abilities. Ensure that when you are working on each phase, you do not worry too much on other phases to avoid making the whole thing overwhelming. Once you are completed with one part, move on the next in line until the whole project is finished.

Prioritize tasks

The other trick is to ensure that you list your tasks in order of priority, starting with the highest to the lowest. It is also important that you define when you intend to work on these tasks according to their order of priority. This ensures that you do not procrastinate important tasks while wasting so much time on tasks that are not urgent.

The methods that you can employ when prioritizing your tasks include:

The Ivy Lee method

This requires that you prepare a to-do list at the end of the day in readiness for the next day. While preparing the to-do list, you have to list down at least six tasks that you would like to complete the following day in order of importance or impact.

The Eisenhower Matrix

This method requires that you categorize each task you have on the basis on whether it is important or not. You also organize them further based on urgency.

That said, these are just two methods that you can employ, but several others have been shown to help in prioritizing tasks. One thing you should bear in mind is that wasting too much time over optimizing your prioritization method risks you getting stuck on what method to use.

SSelect one that works best for your situation or project and use it. If you are not quite certain which method works well, go with the Ivy Lee method and write down a list of 6 tasks to complete at the end of each day.

Determine your productivity cycle

One thing that is important to note is that different people have varying productivity cycles. It often depends on their biological, behavioral, or psychological factors. The best way you can reduce your tendency to procrastinate is to ensure that you identify what your peak times are when you are most productive and then use that to design a schedule when most of your work will be finished.

On the other hand, it is important that you identify your slump times during which your concentration is impaired, and you are least productive. Then use those times to design your schedule for breaks or performing simpler tasks that do not require much focus.

For instance, you may realize that the morning hours are the best times when you focus and concentration at the peak while the times after lunch may be your slump time. In such a case, you can design your schedule such that much of the work that requires focus comes in the morning while after lunch, you can do some leisure activities like working out at the gym or responding to emails among others.

Finally, note that how you handle tasks will better depend on your productivity cycle. For instance, if you are doing creative work, this might be done better early in the day and then other things like emails and phone calls later on. When you do this allocation well, you will be able to leverage every part of the productivity cycle, hence ensuring that you are less likely to postpone.

Set deadlines for yourself

According to research, when you set deadlines, you lower the risk of procrastinating. Setting deadlines play a very critical role as pre-commitment devices that help one plan ahead and stick to their goals by committing to some rate of progress before getting started.

Some of the things that you need to consider when setting

deadlines include:

Are the deadlines concrete?

As we have already discussed, it is clear that when you set concrete deadlines, you increase the chances of following through with them. For instance, if you plan on writing a report, then you can set the deadline to say Friday, 4 PM, which is more concrete than just saying sometime on Friday.

Are your deadlines realistic?

It is important that when setting deadlines, you do it based on the complexity of the task at hand. Ensure that you assess all the activities that a goal has and use that to determine realistically how much time is enough to complete without spending too much unnecessary time.

This is because, if you set the deadline to be too short, then there is a high chance that you will not have adequate time to go over your tasks and this will increase your stress levels. On the other hand, they should not be too long such that you have room to start procrastinating, which is otherwise referred to as Parkinson's Law.

Are your deadlines meaningful?

It is one thing to set a deadline, and it is quite another to abide by them. When setting a deadline on your tasks, it is important that you ensure that you stick to them. This way, you are making them more meaningful to follow through.

One of how you can make them more meaningful is writing them down. You can also bring on someone that will help you become accountable. It is also important that you penalize yourself for not keeping the deadlines and make the punishment more immediate.

That said, every deadline that you set on tasks have to play a role in encouraging you to start working early. This means that, if a deadline is encouraging you to wait for the last minute rush, then it is not a good one. Therefore, whenever possible, it is important that your set deadlines correspond to each step you need to take along the way to achieve the end goal rather than having just a single deadline at the end.

It is also critical that you set proximal goals that you can strive hard at achieving them as you work hard towards achieving the distal goals. Studies have shown that when you use distal goals, you become much more productive and highly motivated compared to when you are working at one huge goal in the future.

Finally, when you create self-imposed deadlines in certain situations that you did not have clearly defined target dates, this can be beneficial in lowering the risk of procrastinating. For instance, if you are at a personal development phase like wanting to start a business or gain fitness, not having a deadline might make you procrastinate to the end of time.

The bottom line is for you to bear in mind that every deadline that you set is effective depending on the scenarios and situations offering them with adequate flexibility. Therefore, if you feel that the deadlines you have set are preventing you from making progress because they cause you to be anxious, then you can avoid them altogether. Just ensure that avoiding deadlines in that situation is the best option rather than just using it as an excuse to procrastinate.

Use timeboxing

This refers to the ability to allocate a specific amount of time to activities that you need to do. This time is referred to as a time box. This is beneficial in such ways as:

It helps ensure that you have allocated adequate time to tasks that you do not like. It means that, if you are supposed to be working out, you do just that without having to replace that with other activities that you consider more appealing.

It helps to avoid dragging tasks that you need to do. For instance, if you dedicate at least an hour to completing the initial design of your book, then you can move on to the next milestone to help you avoid procrastinating for several days stressing over trivial details.

It helps control the time you take on breaks. For instance, you may decide to spend at least 30 minutes on your favorite show after having lunch after which you get back to working on your book description or writing a report. This way, once the 30 minutes are over, you get back to work without really feeling the need to binge watch.

Have a to-do list

When it comes to avoiding procrastination, it helps a lot to write a to-do list at the end of the day or the beginning of each day. It helps break down tasks into smaller actionable activities, prioritize tasks, focus on the high impact tasks first, write reasonable deadlines and sticking with them, and finally tracking your progress to figure out what works and what does not so that you can adjust where necessary.

To create a to-do list, you can use a variety of techniques like the pen-and-paper method or other apps that are available on the market. The point is for you to try out various ways to arrive at one that works best for you. However, ensure that you do not end up over prioritizing the approach itself. If it is necessary, you can always reevaluate and modify the approach as you go along.

Establish streaks

One of the best ways to motivate you is by using streaks or chains that you do not wish to break. For instance, you might decide each day that you will not waste time on social media or you draft the methodology section of your thesis counts, and you add it to your streak.

But the question is, "how do you keep track of your streaks?" the truth is, you have to make them meaningful so that you can maintain it and boost your motivation to keep working without putting things off to another day.

One method that you can use to keep track of streaks is Seinfeld strategy. This involves marking a red X on the calendar each time you complete your daily tasks or goals. On the other hand, if you are using a mobile app for time management, there is a high chance that there are settings that allow you to keep track of your streaks.

Gamify your habits

This refers to integrating certain elements derived from games such as the accumulation of points and competing with other people. It goes a long way in boosting your level of motivation so that you work hard towards your goals. When this is implemented correctly, it can be a very powerful tool in getting you to stop procrastinating.

In this case, you can decide that when you work on a certain task successfully and within the required time limit, you get several points. If you procrastinate, then you lose a certain number of points. The good thing with this strategy is that you can try various ways of implementing it until you find one that works well for you and helps you combat procrastination.

Establish a routine

This is something that you can choose to establish on a daily, weekly, or monthly basis to help you complete important tasks in a timely fashion. Ensure that while establishing your daily routines, you consider your productivity cycles. Simply means that each routine is unique for each person. It is especially important for those people with an erratic sleep schedule and is prone to sleep deprivation, causing them to become more prone to procrastination.

Commit to having no "zero days"

A zero-day refers to a day that you do nothing towards advancing towards your goals. When you decide to have no days that end without you doing something meaningful towards accomplishing your goals, there is a high chance that you will begin to draw closer and closer to your dream. Therefore, if you have so many goals in mind, it is important that you implement this approach so that each passing day you become one step closer to your goals.

Plan well for future contingencies

One of the major reasons why people fail to overcome their procrastination habits is because they fail to plan ahead of time for situations that might cause them to postpone activities. You can mitigate this by simply creating a strong implementation intention which you can do by identifying areas you struggle so that you can successfully self-regulate. This way, you can ensure that you come up with the right goals that are aimed at strengthening your habits if you were to find yourself in such situations by chance.

For instance, if you find that one if the major contributing factors to your procrastination even when you know you should be working is having a friend over, and you find it hard to turn them down; you can come up with a plan that will help you turn them down so that you can stick to your routine. You can arrange to meet them another time, most preferably your slump times.

Increase your energy levels

One of the best ways to stop procrastinating is ensuring that before you get started on your daily tasks, you are refreshed and strong enough to push through. If you start working when you are tired, the chances are that you will procrastinate. Some of the ways that you can ensure that you stay energetic include:

Getting sufficient sleep

If you do not get enough sleep, your focus and level of concentration will be greatly affected, increasing your chances of procrastinating. Ensure that you get sufficient sleep so that you are more productive enough to tackle both difficult and simple tasks ahead of you.

Drink enough water

If you want to improve your level of concentration, it is critical that you stay hydrated. You can do this by drinking a glass of water from time to time while working in the office.

Eat a healthy meal

There is no way you can work on something serious when you are on an empty stomach. Your brain functions on glucose, and if the glucose levels are far too low, then the chances are that you will not be able to focus and reason. Therefore, before you get started, have something to bite to boost your glucose levels and cause you to concentrate on the important task ahead.

Exercise

As they say, "too much work and no play make Jack a dull boy." Well, this is true. Engaging in physical activity has been shown to make people feel better; stay focused and have the right attitude to face the day. Start each day with a few workout exercises and see the difference that makes on your performance at work.

Get rid of distractions

The environment that we work is very important in contributing to our productivity. If your working space is cluttered, this can be a big cause of distraction, making you susceptible to procrastination. Getting rid of distractions increases your concentration.

When I started working, my office desk was set close to the reception. It was a corridor where everyone coming into the office, walked through. Additionally, I was seated right at my bosses' door, which was very distracting, especially when he has guests and discussions going on, and the door is wide open. Trust me; I could barely concentrate on what I was supposed to be working on.

Maybe you have a different kind of distraction like working next to call center section with all the phones ringing and people talking over the phone. Alternatively, that colleague that cannot seem to stop telling you stories of how their weekend went down. Alternatively, maybe the television is on, and you cannot seem to function well multitasking.

According to research, there is evidence that shows that people with low levels if self-control is more likely to multitask. Therefore, ensure that you improve your working environment to suit the kind of task you are doing and the level of concentration each task needs. If it is cluttered, clear up your space and organize your office desk so that your attention does not shift from what is most important to what is going on around you. This will make it easier for you to concentrate and perform better in what you are doing.

If your working environment is the cause for your procrastination, you can change it. You can choose to go to the library or the coffee shop or sit by the swimming pool among other places that draw your concentration to the task at hand. If you work from home, it can be helpful to separate each area based on the functions in your life, such as dining, sleeping, and working. This allows you to effectively make a mental switch when you get into the "work mode."

Get rid of bottlenecks

Bottlenecks refer to certain tasks that are causing you to procrastinate on important tasks. In other words, you cannot start working on these important tasks without getting rid of bottlenecks.

They are referred to as bottlenecks for quite several reasons. For instance, for you to start data analysis, you have to have collected all the data first. It could also be because of mental perspective in which you would like to complete one task first before moving on to another.

If you realize that some of the tasks are bottlenecks and are the reason why you keep postponing certain tasks, it is critical that you find a way to get rid of them. Some of the ways to do this include:

Just getting it done

This is one of the most obvious ways of approaching this. You can do this by employing some of the strategies that we have already discussed earlier in this book. However, if you still find yourself stuck on the bottlenecks, change your strategy until you have everything working out smoothly.

Modify it

In some instances, if you can change the bottlenecks in such a way that they allow you to focus on the real deal, and then you've got to do it.

Delegate it

In some cases, you will find that some of these bottlenecks

blocking the way for important tasks can be down by someone else. All you have to do is delegate them to someone that can handle it so that you have peace of mind to concentrate on what makes you draw nearer to your set goals.

Eliminate it completely

Sometimes, you might realize that something that was a bottleneck is not worth doing anymore, and you eliminate it, especially when it is getting in the way of progressing on important tasks.

That said, you have to understand that different techniques of dealing with bottlenecks will work better under different circumstances. The most important thing is for you to figure out what method works best in your case and helps you fast-track the process.

Avoid a perfectionist mindset

As we have already discussed earlier, perfectionism refers to the tendency of viewing anything as flawed and unacceptable. This is the biggest contributor to procrastination. It is this kind of mindset that can cause you to delay from getting started, keep revising your work endlessly, and avoid making your work accessible to the public among others.

You have to realize that the very reason why you keep postponing is that you have a strong desire to attain perfection. Acceptance is the very first step to dealing with an issue like this. Once you are aware and have accepted it as the real cause, then it is time that you begin to internalize that we are ourselves imperfect, and so is our work, and that is okay. It is important that you shake off the fear of making mistakes so that you can make progress and learn from those mistakes.

If you have not started working on your project yet, then it is high time that you started and accepted that no matter how hard or how long you work on it, it can never be perfect. Try to get something done as a starting point even if the quality is not the best at that point. On the other hand, if you keep revising your work over and over again, try to get a second opinion from someone you trust so that you have an honest opinion based on their evaluation of the work's quality.

Visualize your future self

Did you know that if you start to see yourself having achieved your goals and living your dream, you will lower the tendency of postponing? Well, this is true. Visualizing your future increases the degree to which you care about your dreams and achieving them, how much you care about the consequences of your actions as well as the perceived value of future outcomes of your work.

Seeing your future self is often referred to as an episodic future thinking. It can be how you will feel a couple of months from today, having your dream house or having achieved the current project you have been working on. While doing this, it is important that you focus on both positive outcomes of pushing through with your commitment; and negative outcomes of procrastinating.

You can visualize your future either in first person or third person. In other words, you can start seeing future events as though they were already happening in the present through your eyes, or you can perceive them from an observer's eye. Irrespective of what option you go for, it is critical that you commit to your visualization by making it as detailed as possible. The more you become connected to it, the more you will be motivated to work towards making that a reality, and the more you will overcome procrastination.

Identify someone to hold you accountable

One of the most important things when it comes to overcoming procrastination is having someone that will hold you accountable for your actions. This can be anyone you trust from a friend you share information with about your new project to a colleague at work that gets your struggles. You can bet such that if you have completed the work by the end of a certain time, then you give them $20. The better they can assist you, the more motivated you will be to completing the task at hand.

The rewards do not necessarily have to be tangible or have a penalty associated with it. Sometimes all it takes is caring enough about their opinion. In most cases, what matters is having them be proud of your actions or progress and avoiding disappointments.

Seek favorable peer influence

Have you ever realized that the people you spend too much time with have a huge impact on the person you become? For instance, when you surround yourself with people who work hard to pursue their goals, you stay motivated to do the same too. Their actions and way of life encourage you to be accountable for your actions. That is what I refer to as a positive influence.

On the other hand, if you surround yourself with people who tend to spend so much of their time doing things that do not matter or add any value to their goals and dreams; they can cause you to do the same. You find yourself procrastinating on the important stuff and doing things that do not matter. Their influence causes you to disregard the value of your goals. This is what I refer to as a negative influence.

As such, it is important that you seek a positive influence by spending time with people who make you a better person at what you do. They are the people that will be happy to cheer you on as you go on to pursue your goals. It is also critical that you avoid negative peer influence.

Chapter 5 Strategies that Can Help You Change

If you are going to overcome procrastination, it is important that you understand the stages that you have to go through to break this habit. This uses the stages of the change model that helps people learn how they can get rid of self-destructive behaviors. These stages include: pre-contemplation, contemplation, preparation, action, maintenance, and termination.

It is very important to know the stage of change you are in currently. This ensures that you use specific strategies that will help you to effectively take you through that stage and into the next level of personal recovery. If you fail to use strategies that are specific to your stage of change, the chances are that you will stall your recovery. It explains the reason why so many people who have gone through rehabilitation have not been able to s shake off successfully their old self-destructive had.

Stage 1: Pre-contemplation

This is a stage that is characterized by a lack of awareness of your problem. During this stage, you do not have any intention to act in the foreseeable future in an attempt to fix your problem. In other words, when you are at this stage, you are not ready to change. It is mainly because you have not accepted that you have a problem. You are simply in denial.

One thing that you have to understand is that if you are at this stage, it is important that you have factual information about your procrastination habit. This way, you will be able to understand the real consequences of your actions so that you are better equipped to make informed choices about whether or not to quit your habit of procrastination.

You could also discuss your problem and concerns with a therapist or a friend who can offer you accurate feedback on how your procrastination habit affects you and the people around you. They will actively help challenge your denial so that you can work towards recovery. The worst thing is allowing your procrastination habits to cause pain and even death to the people you care most for. When you start working on your recovery, you will be inspired to get back on the right track.

Stage 2: Contemplation

Now, you are already aware that you have a problem and you intend to do something about it. However, the problem is that your intentions at this point are still vague because you do not have any idea what to do about it.

At this stage, what is going through your mind are the do's and don'ts of continuing the self-destructive behavior, giving up altogether. In other words, you are at a stage in which you are undecided. It is important that you speak to a professional therapist concerning your thoughts on how the change will come about.

You should ensure that you use your therapist to bounce off the merits of continuing your procrastination habits or even quitting altogether so that you can make an informed decision. Seeking the help of a professional assures you that you will be able to think through all these issues more productively. It also ensures that while you do that, you do not pass any judgments so that you accept yourself the way you are.

Stage 3: Preparation

This stage involves you having a plan on what you intend to do so that you can deal with the problem of procrastination. At this point, you have decided that quitting the habit of procrastination is the way to go and are acting. One thing that you have to do is to gather adequate quality information on your procrastination change program and join people who have struggled with a similar habit and have been able to overcome.

Stage 4: Action

When you are at this stage, you start acting on your plan or course of action in an attempt to overcome your procrastination habit. In other words, at this point, you are already changing. It is, therefore, important that you surround yourself with people who can actively help facilitate your attendance to your procrastination change program.

Ensure that you can engage the people that mean a lot to you, such as your friends and family to help support you through the process. Such group sessions not only help you share your problems with others but also inspire you to work towards addressing the issue of hearing what others have gone through because of their procrastination habits. Such support is important in helping you keep track of your progress.

Stage 5: Maintenance

At this point, you are no longer procrastinating. However, you continue to take the necessary actions that you need to ensure that you do not slowly allow procrastination back in your life. In other words, what you are doing is continually reinforcing change, support, and encouragement to keep going.

You have to realize that, when you are at this stage, the temptations may loom but not as strong as they used to be. This means that you have to enlist the support of your close friends, colleagues, and family to keep you accountable for your actions and decisions. They will ensure that you remain on the right track to recovery so that you not only consolidate but also internalize the change so that it comes naturally.

Note that there are so many things that might try to undermine your progress. But you have to remember that you are not yet completely out of the woods and hence it is not time for you to be complacent. Trying to convince yourself that you have been so good and just one procrastination will not make a difference is a recipe for disaster, and you will find yourself right back at the pre-contemplation stage!

One interesting fact that you have to bear in mind is that many people often go through several cycles of change before they can successfully overcome their self-destructing habits. Think about alcoholics, smokers and others who after trying and failing many times, they come out the other side free of their habits! In the same way, you can take your procrastination habit as a sport or weight loss plan that you have to work hard to eventually get where you are going.

Stage 6: Termination

This is the point at which procrastination has been eliminated and is no longer a problem. It is important to note that for some people, getting to this stage can be tricky because they risk relapsing to their old habits. In other words, you will need to stick to the maintenance stage indefinitely.

Additionally, the amount of time and condition to overcoming procrastination varies from one individual to another. Therefore, while there are those that will overcome their behaviors fast, there are those that will take a significant amount of time to get there finally. Nonetheless, the longer you stick to your plan by sticking to positive habits, the easier for you to keep going, and the better you get at overcoming procrastination.

Experiment and Reassess

One thing that is important to note is that there is no single cure for procrastination. This is mainly because procrastination is a complex problem in which different people will benefit from varying strategies and solutions.

This means that there is no one right way to stopping procrastination. Instead, the best approach is one that helps you deal with the issue by first understanding your habit as much as you can. Then you can try applying various approaches and solutions to it until you find one that works best for you.

Start your day on fire

If you are going to enjoy everything you do, you have to start the day on fire. When you are pursuing your dream, you will go through seasons of struggle and victory. One day, things are very exciting to you, and the next day, you are bored and are tempted to procrastinate. To overcome the temptation to procrastinate, it is important that you express your deepest desire, purpose, and passion. If you are going to work hard at attaining your goals, then you have to be willing to live in your passion.

Yes, you want to see your business succeed or career take a new direction. To do this, you have to say the words that set you on fire and then take a step further to light the fire in your career, business, and team. In other words, you have to put passion first before practicality.

Four years ago, a friend of mine leaped faith to start their own business. It was a huge step, and she started by writing her vision, mission, and value statements. Each year, she read through them and made a couple of improvements, but that did not seem to be enough. Then I advised her to start reading them aloud each day, first thing in the morning, and things began to take root.

The points are:

Vocalizing

When you start reading your goals and dream out aloud

each morning, this hits both sides of your brain. Notice that the left side of the brain is logical whiles the right side if more emotional and motivational. In other words, the left side of the brain justifies what you tell it and tries to create negative resistance. Therefore, by reading your goals, dreams, or tasks aloud, what you are simply doing is unifying both the right and the left side to work together towards realizing those dreams.

Practicing daily

It is important to note that motivation is more like exercising, means that the more you work out, the more you become stronger and fit. It also goes for stirring up the passion within you each morning. Think of today as the most important day of your life. Simply make a fresh start and turn towards the right direction.

First things first

According to Stephen Covey, the author of "*Seven Habits of Highly effective people*," you have to be willing to do the first things first if you are going to achieve your goals. This means that you begin every single day with the things that matter most. In fact, during the very first two hours of the day, spend it pursuing positive and nourishing ideas. In other words, rather than starting the day with the newspaper, emails, gossip, and social media, among other things, start it with what makes your dreams come true!

Start your day by reading your goals and mission out loud. This will make you feel dynamic, energized, and will stir the internal fire burning within you to come alive on the outside. You have to go the extra mile to feed that fire as often as possible.

Look out for the things that come in to let the fire out of your day and avoid them. These are the things that cause you to want to procrastinate on those dreams. It may be a customer that is always complaining, a coworker that is distracting you with meaningless stories and gossip or a traffic jam that makes you get to work late among other things.

Realize that it is time to pay attention to your vision. Think of yourself as a Marathoner, if you stumble and fall, you get up, dust yourself, take a deep breath, refocus, and start running in the right direction. The truth is, it does not matter how many times we make mistakes, procrastinate, or fail to meet deadlines, what truly matters is being able to pick ourselves up quickly and work fast on recovery.

Start by creating a one-line version of your dream or goals so that whenever life tries to throw you off balance with the temptation of procrastinating, you stand up straight, balance and take a shot. Take deep breaths three times and say the one-line version of your goal. This way, you will feel a strong wave coming from within you to relight the fire of your passion. You will feel a renewal of your energy and commitment to get to work and push through the path to success.

One thing that comes to kill your fire is procrastination. It tells you that your goal is what you have to do rather than what you dream of being. It tells you that you are what society wants you to be rather than what you want to be. It causes you to forget your mission and dreams. It pushes you to start resisting and hating what you love doing in the first place.

If you are going to increase your productivity, then you have to quiet the voice within that tells you that you have to do something. "You have to go to work, you have to work out, and you have to go to a doctor's appointment and so on." That is the voice that will cause you to burn out and hate your work. Stick to what you do because you feel passionate about it and watch what the result will be like. The point is, start your day on fire and keep it burning clean.

Chapter 6 The Power of Nice

The role of self-criticism in procrastination

Self-criticism is one of the key motivators of fear. Whenever we fail, one of the most unpleasant things is criticizing ourselves for allowing failure. In most cases, the kind of self-criticism we pass on ourselves is similar to pointing a gun to our head and hoping that the situation will make us stop being complacent. We often think to ourselves, if I do not do this, I will beat myself, or I must force myself to do this otherwise that.

Well, this approach may work to a certain extent. However, there are many disadvantages associated with this approach. The truth is, when we constantly pass threats on ourselves, we are simply stirring up anxiety and worry, which in turn undermines our productivity. You have to understand that pressure does nothing but hinder you from performing at your best.

Secondly, self-criticism has been shown to lead to self-handicapping. This means that we self-sabotage our performance just so that we can save our ego whenever we fail. In other words, you aim at sabotaging yourself so that if you fail, you avoid feeling unworthy by just blaming that the reason why you failed is that you did not try or did not have adequate time to work.

In her book "*Self-Compassion*," Kristin Neff explains that there is a less likelihood of self-critics attaining their goals as a result of self-handicapping strategy. In one study, college students were asked to describe their academic, health, and social related goals and give a report of the progress they had made towards achieving these goals. The results showed that self-critics made less progress and that they often procrastinated.

From these findings, it is clear that one of the reasons why people procrastinate is because of self-criticism. However, let's think of this for a second "what if we criticize ourselves for procrastinating?" once we have procrastinated, is there a chance that this could keep us from repeating the same in future?

Well, the answer to these questions is NO! According to research, there is evidence that shows self-forgiveness after procrastinating goes a long way in lowering procrastination. In other words, when you spend too much time beating yourself up for procrastinating, you are not adding any value. You are making things even worse.

The role of self-compassion in procrastination

According to research, there are so many ways in which you can use self-compassion to boost your motivation and performance. All these work well in lowering your chances of procrastinating. Self-compassionate people have been shown to experience less anxiety and worry, something that, in turn, allows them to take more risks and act more. When you have less fear of the unknown, you will not require a plausible excuse for failure and hence fewer chances of self-handicapping.

So, the question is, why are that person who are self-compassionate experience less failure? The truth is, at the back of their minds, they know that even if they fail, in the end, they will be just fine. In other words, they do not have to be afraid of self-punishment. Rather, they understand that people fuck up and they forgive themselves for the mistakes they make.

Such people allow themselves to experience failure like something that is neutral or even better - positive! Research has shown that people who have self-compassion often perceive failure as something worth embracing instead of fearing. They view it as an opportunity to grow, learn, and become better at what they do rather than seeing it as a measure of their self-worth.

This explains the reason why such people are willing and able to take risks and trying out new things without necessarily having to feel anxious about punishments in case they fail. Realize that self-compassion is creating a safe surrounding that allows you to feel safe, calm, and confident. When you allow yourself to operate from that place, then you will not have a reason to fear failure or feel the need to procrastinate just so that you can keep your ego.

Learn to forgive yourself

One research paper published in the Journal of Personality and individual difference explains that self-forgiveness plays a critical role in lowering the occurrence if procrastination. One thing that you have to bear in mind is that forgiveness is not something that we do for people. It is something that we do it for ourselves so that we can get well and move on with our life.

When you choose to forgive yourself for procrastinating a task in the present, what you are doing in effect is that you are lowering your chances of procrastinating in the future. This is a relationship that is mediated by negative effects that by expressing self-forgiveness, you lower procrastination and in effect, reduce negative emotions.

The truth is, you should not feel bad about the choices that you made at first. The most important thing is for you to accept that you are not perfect and are prone to making mistakes. The best thing you do to yourself is forgiveness.

When we fail to express self-forgiveness, then we risk avoiding motivation and hence increase our likelihood of procrastinating more in the future.

That said, it is correct to note that self-criticism causes us to procrastinate more while self-compassion causes us to procrastinate less. Therefore, if you are going to stop procrastination, it is important that you do these;

First, forgive yourself for procrastinating. When you choose to beat yourself up for the mistakes that you have made, you make the whole situation worse than it already is. Situations happen and cause us to procrastinate, and that is natural. Each one of us has done it, and there is no point being so overly critical of you. It is also okay if you felt a little guilt and dissatisfaction. Rather than trying to sweep these feelings under the carpet, acknowledge, accept, and resolve them so that you can do better in the future.

Secondly, develop genuine self-compassion. This serves as a great start, especially when you have procrastinated. It is the thing that tells you that you can do better and have lots of room to improve. When you have genuine compassion, the truth is that you will procrastinate less, live a healthy life, and achieve more as you go along.

Chapter 7 The Art of Emotion Surfing

Learn to surf your emotions

Procrastination comes with a wave of emotions. However, the essential way of overcoming procrastination is effectively regulating these emotions. Whenever you dread obligations, it is these emotions that drag our feet into completing them. It is quite unfortunate that most people confuse their tasks with emotional suffering. Yes, the task at hand may be complicated and hard and may cause you to despair or feel anxious, but it is not meant for your suffering.

When we face tasks that are challenging we become more challenge-averse. All these negative emotions and reservations add up, and they cause us to try hard to avoid doing these tasks altogether just so that we do not experience the wave of emotional suffering. The trick here is for you to adjust your task, and you will begin to see that your mood will change.

"You can't stop the waves, but you can learn to surf."
– Jon Kabat-Zinn

One thing that you have to note is that emotions are just like waves because one minute they are here and the other, they are gone. Imagine an ocean, sometimes, the waves are small, and in other times, they are very big. Irrespective of what they do, the truth is that the waves will keep coming. Therefore, if you are in the water and are getting closer to the shore, what you need to do is surf them so that you do not end up being pulled under the waves. It is something that can be scary and painful and often leaves us feeling powerless.

The same applies to our emotions. The trick is to learn how to surf them so that we do not end up being crushed by them. Here are some of the best ways you can learn to surf your emotions;

Start from the basics

One thing that you have to realize is that if you are going to face your procrastination habits, the first thing is to learn the basics. It is just the same way as surfing a five-meter wave. You cannot do it if you do not start with the basics. The point is, start by observing and learning from people who have been able to go through what you are going through and come out the other side successful.

Learn from them how they do it. For some reason, it is important that we know how to handle our emotions from the onset. We have to know what to do with them when they come. Understand that surfing your emotions is a skill just like any other. Therefore, you have to understand the various types of emotions, the purpose of their existence, the ways you can navigate through them and then mastering the art of dealing with them effectively.

Get your feet wet

Once you already know the basics, then it is high time you got into the water. The first thing that you learn when you get into the water is how to paddle out beyond the breaking point of the waves. You hang out at that point for several hours trying to get a sense of the waves, their size, and speed. In other words, what you are trying to do at that point is familiarizing yourself so that you can know what the best way to respond is.

This similar concept applies to our emotions. When we understand the basics, we need to get into the water so that we can watch them coming and going. You could be anxious about the task ahead and are tempted to procrastinate. However, the trick is for you to recognize what you are feeling and even name the emotional feelings you are experiencing, whether it is sadness, anxiety, happiness, or fear, among others. That places you ion a better position to surf through them. When we accurately tell what emotional feelings we are experiencing, only then can we be able to surf through them with a high degree of accuracy and precision.

Understand the weather

If there is anything that you should appreciate is that emotions will not just happen, just like waves will not magically appear. They are often a result of a certain condition and pressure in the surrounding. When you understand well the area you are surfing in; then you can easily avoid accidents that are likely to happen.

The emotional feelings you are experiencing do not just come out of the blues. They have a definite source. In other words, every feeling has a reason for its existence, and it is important that we understand their source. When we feel anxious, it may be because we are closer to the deadline, and we have not completed what we were supposed to do. If it is anger, it may be because of some injustice; pride may be from an achievement that brings us happiness or fear coming from danger and believing that we may not be able to deal with a certain situation.

The truth is, in most cases, we may not know where these feelings are coming from or even what the trigger is. However, it is critical that we wear our detective hat and get out to investigate what underlies it, what the thought behind it was, and the thing that just happened in your life.

Make friends with the waves

One thing that is important to note is that we do not choose the waves in the ocean. They will keep coming even after we have stopped surfing for the day. When you try to fight them or stop them, this may be a hopeless cause. Rather than trying to stop them, it is important that we try to learn how to ride them so that we can get past the breaking point and safely get to the shore.

Indeed, there will always be times when our feelings have weighed us down enough, and we wish that they could finally go away. Here is the truth, the more you try to fight your emotions, the stronger they will become. The only way you are going to get through them is by accepting them, allow them to flow and pay attention to what they have to say. Trust me; there is always a message in every emotional feeling.

Harness the power of the emotion

Once you have mastered the art of surfing the waves, then it becomes very easy to move from one point to another. When you get good at it, you will know how to tap into its energy and power so that you can do the things that you want.

The emotional feelings you are experiencing are your guide in life. It is through these emotions that you are equipped with exactly what you need so that you can effectively and efficiently deal with a certain situation. When we are angry, we get motivated to work hard to make things right. Fear brings us endurance, and pride gives us the confidence to strive for more. These gifts are always at our disposal, but the trick is to learn how to tap into them and leverage them to our advantage.

Surf your emotions like a guru

If you are already in the water and we see waves approaching but do nothing about it, the chances are that they will pass us by or end up swallowing us. In other words, with every coming wave, there are three things we can do;

choose to catch it or stand up and surf it or allow it to go. The truth is whatever it is that we do; it is a choice we have made.

In the same manner, when we experience emotional waves in our life, we have a choice to make; either explode or direct that energy into figuring out the best solution. In other words, we can either face them and keep going or give up on them and run. The truth is, every emotion comes with a suggestion on how we need to act, and in fact, there is always more than one way. The key here is to study yourself, accept and appreciate the emotional feelings you are experiencing and then choose what suggestion works best for your situation. Whatever it is that you choose, ask yourself whether it helps you get what you want.

That said, one thing that you have to bear in mind is that overcoming procrastination and handling emotional feelings it brings is not something that you can learn overnight. The first thing is for you to learn the basics, then start practicing and give yourself enough time to develop the new skills. Yes, they are not the simplest of skills to learn mainly because they involve a change of habit. However, once you get over the first hurdle, you start seeing the benefits and appreciate that it was worth all the hard work.

Chapter 8 Establish a Strong Willpower

According to research studies, there is a growing body of evidence that shows that for one to lead a happy and successful life, they need to have strong willpower and a sense of self-control. The most persuasive of this evidence include:

The marshmallow experiment in which the scientist gave 4-year old children a choice of a marshmallow now and the other choice is if they could wait for 15 minutes. The performance of the children is tracked as they grew into adulthood. What was interesting was that those children that resisted the temptation achieved impeccable academic excellence, better health, and enjoyed happy marriages. The scientist concluded that when one has a delayed gratification, it acts as a protective buffer against vulnerabilities in life.

The second experiment is one in which 1000 children were monitored right from birth to the time when they were 32 years old. What was interesting was that childhood self-control was directly linked to personal finances, physical health, substance dependence, and criminal offenses, among others. It was still true even with the equation of such factors as social class and level of intelligence. When sibling pairs are compared, the sibling with lower self-control was shown to have poor results despite their social background.

So, when all is said and done, what is it that you can do to improve your willpower, lower procrastination and boost your productivity?

To explain this better, let us consider some facts about the muscles in the body. When we exercise, the muscles get stronger. However, when they are overworked, the chances are that they will become weaker unless given time to recover adequately.

What is interesting is that this also applies to willpower. One study research participants were asked not to think about a white bear. The truth is, such thought-suppression tasks have a great impact on our willpower, but most importantly, they require self-control. Once they had completed the task, they were required to limit their beer intake during a taste test mainly because soon after, they were supposed to participate in a driving test. These participants were said to have taken a lot of beer compared to those that did not take part in the thought-suppression task.

In another study, people were asked to try as much as they could to suppress their feelings as they watched a very upsetting movie. What was interesting is that these people gave up so soon compared to people that watched the movie freely without the need to suppress their feelings.

You will realize that, in all these instances, people experienced lots of difficulties slogging through tough tasks whenever their willpower had been depleted. The good news is that, if you think that your willpower is the reason why you keep procrastinating, and then you can improve it in several ways.

Do not keep yourself in a constant state of depleted willpower

One of the best ways you can build your muscles includes weight-lifting. However, if a friend asked you to help them move their furniture soon after weight lifting, the truth is that you will not spend more than 30 minutes doing this exercise. This is mainly because your muscles will be too tired to do a good job. Additionally, you cannot spend hours weightlifting without taking breaks in between workouts.

This similar principle holds when it comes to willpower. While it a great way to build your willpower by exercising self-control, not taking breaks in between can cause a depletion of your resolve.

This explains the reason why in sports, coaches often distinguish stretch and comfort zones. In other words, if you are comfortable running at least 10-minute mile, increasing your pace will likely put you in a stretch zone. However, if you are going to improve your performance, then you have to be able to balance between the two. It means that staying in one zone continuously is not a very good idea as you may risk injury. The same thing applies to your willpower.

Use your imagination

One of the most powerful techniques of improving your willpower is through imagination. The truth is that the body responds to imagined situations just as it does ones it experiences. For instance, if you imagine lying flat on the beach and listening to the lapping of the waves at the shore, the truth is that the body will respond to this by simply allowing itself to relax. If you imagine not completing that report in time, then your body will tense up, and you will be anxious and less productive. This is what you can do to build your willpower-imagination!

According to willpower experts, dieting is one of the ways one keeps them in a chronic state of depletion. Because of this, the person dieting will experience minor irritations to an intense longing for rest or something to eat. However, with imagination, you can blunt the feelings that erode your self-control.

In one study, the research participants were asked to watch a movie with a bowl of candy close by. One group was asked to imagine that they had eaten as much as they needed and the other group was asked to imagine that they had eaten none and the third group had decided to eat their share later.

What was interesting was that the first group ate more than the other two groups. When they were finally offered the opportunity to eat their candy, those that had imagined that they would eat later ate way less than the other two groups.

The same thing applies to procrastination. If you start imagining taking on your tasks very early in the morning., chances are that your willpower will be so strong as to allow you do your tasks and delay the urge of reading emails, chatting on Facebook or doing other tasks that are not of immediate importance.

Think of something else

Did you know that you can use your imagination to keep unwanted thoughts at bay? When you tell yourself that you will not think of a polar bear, what is interesting is that that will be the thing that you will seem not to shake off your mind.

The question that comes to your mind is, "but how do I avoid thinking of the bear? Alternatively, how do I not think of chatting on Facebook?" The truth is you simply need to train your mind to occupy itself with something else. In other words, each time you want to procrastinate that task, think of doing it instead. Each time that unwanted though threatens to intrude your mind, think of something pleasant that will instead place you at the driver's seat of your thoughts.

Build good habits because you will need them when you are down

We have already seen how stress and anxiety can impact your productivity. As it turns out, this also hurts your willpower. It simply depletes it little by little until you do not have any more willpower in you.

One thing that you have to understand is that when people are anxious or stressed, they tend falling back to their old habits - irrespective of whether these habits are helpful or harmful. In most cases, this is not a conscious thought or choice. Instead, the reason why they choose to go back to these habits is that they are not thinking straight and are in a stressed state.

For instance, let us say that you have an important business presentation very early in the morning. Based on how you give the presentation, you will be offered a promotion at the company. The truth is, this is a very stressful situation which the body responds to by releasing cortisol, a stress hormone.

However, what will be your response? Well, cortisol is well known to boost food cravings, especially of carbs. When you handle your stress in such a manner, you risk being obese, having cardiovascular diseases, or suffering from obesity. You may think of taking alcohol to lower your stress, but then you stand a risk of becoming an alcoholic in the long-run. This means that, whenever you have stress, you will risk falling back to these habits.

The good thing is that knowledge is power. In other words, if you deal with your stress-induced increase in cortisol, the chances are that you will be able to manage your sugar and alcohol cravings. Therefore, it is important that whenever you are under duress, you respond to such stressors by making healthy choices like visualization, listening to calming music, working out among other activities. The more you strengthen healthy habits, the more likely that you will fall back to them when you are stressed.

Take one step at a time

One of the reasons why people despair is because they feel that the goals they are pursuing are so enormous and overwhelming. It is not often because they lack willpower. When you feel that your goals are too overwhelming is to try and break them into small chunks that you can focus on with little pressure. When you line them up in a sequence, you are guaranteed to attaining success in each because you will take one chunk at a time.

Someone once said that their job has lots of pressure and

tight deadlines, but they manage. Their secret is to break the large elephant into smaller pieces and then eating each piece at a time without necessarily looking up to check how much is left to go.

This is quite similar to when preparing for a marathon. If you want to complete your race, the trick is for you to run as many laps as you can. Then purpose on adding one lap to your race every week. When you do this, you will be amazed how much progress you will make by the time the actual marathon starts in a couple of months.

The good thing with this strategy is that you will not only have success but also are certain that your willpower will never run out. As you move from one micro-goal to another, there is so much satisfaction you will feel making all other remaining small goals easy to tackle. Eventually, when you reach the final goal, there is a high chance that you will feel a strong sense of abundance and energy rather than exhaustion.

Be yourself

It is important to note that for you to suppress your normal personality, habits, and preferences; you have to exert lots of effort. What is not surprising is that this also causes a depletion of your willpower. Research studies have shown that when you exert such kind of self-control for the sake of pleasing others, you will run out of willpower compared to people who hold on to their internal desires and dreams. The truth is people pleasers often are at a disadvantage as far as willpower is concerned. The secret to being productive is staying true to yourself and being comfortable in your skin and abilities.

Do not expose yourself to temptations, and if you do, have a plan

If you are going to be productive and reach your goals, you have to ensure that you get rid of everything that might stand in the way of your achievements and realization of goals. If there are things that make you procrastinate on the most important tasks, then try to avoid them as much as possible. It is just like when you are trying to lose weight, and someone comes to the house with so many candy bars. The trick is to have them locked away where you cannot access.

In the same way, if you have distractions, social media and other things that take away your attention and time from what matters most, then you have to be willing to get rid of them or at least have a plan to handle them whenever they come your way. When you know what your weaknesses are, this allows you to enact an effective plan.

Chapter 9 Simplify Your Life

One of the things that so many people fail to understand is that working too hard can be counterproductive. Yes, that is right! You have to realize that the secret to having fantastic productivity is not just about hard work. It is about working smart and making your life as simplified as possible so that you can focus on what truly matters.

So, what does it mean to work smart and live a simplified life?

If you are going to be very productive in what you do, one thing that you have to learn how to say NO! Turning something down is a sign that you are not giving your all just so that you can work, work and work. Sometimes, all you have to tell that friend is that you will not be able to hang out with them today because your schedule is full. Meeting your deadlines should not take away your happiness and sunshine. The trick is for you to learn to prioritize tasks so that once you have completed the most important ones, you can take a break to breathe.

Realize that people are not going to respect at the workplace if all you do is say yes to everything. It would help if you learned how to be assertive. This is mainly because, if you choose to stretch yourself too thin, the chances are that the quality of work you will deliver will be poor.

Simplifying your life is about ensuring that your focus is narrowed down to things that matter most and then learning to let go of all else. Assess the activities in your work and determine which ones are very important. Determine also those that you need to be doing, but you do them as a tradition or habit. Say no to these activities so that you can focus on the most important tasks and complete them in time while still delivering high quality.

To work smart is to know when to take breaks throughout your day. For instance, after working for 2 hours continuously, your concentration might have started going down and hence the need for a short break or even taking a walk around campus to get fresh air before getting back. Yes, it may be heroic to work for 6 hours non-stop without even getting off your chair for a second, but it is not effective. The level of productivity might be lower than that of someone that works two hours and takes regular breaks in between.

Take some time to stretch, breath, or even regroup. If you are working from home, you can do some exercises to increase your concentration. Just getting off that computer can help you lower the stress levels. Breaks are supposed to be just that - breaks! If you are still half-working while on break, then the truth is that it will not yield the same positive effects on your level of productivity. Ensure that breaks are true breaks where you relax away from work.

You have to realize that you do not need to accomplish everything at once. That is the reason why people make schedules or to-do lists. If you allow yourself to get too busy on conflicting priorities, then you might not be able to get quality work done, and you might end up procrastinating on what matters most. In other words, you will find yourself having lots of things to do but NEVER getting any done.

Rather than stressing yourself about too much work on your plate, take a deep breath and relax. Choose your top priorities or high-impact tasks and focus on them. The truth is, the more you live in peace with the fact that you cannot get everything done at once, the happier you will be, and the more productive you get.

You will end up less effective if you try to juggle up everything at the same time. The truth is, when you have your attention spread across many tasks at the same time, you will not deliver everything at the right time, and you will end up frustrated and anxious.

The other way to simplify your life is to ensure that you have time each day to unwind. You can use that time to go to the gym, or even watch your favorite show. The essence of having technology is so that we can still be contacted throughout the day and night. Taking time to clear your head goes a long way in helping you think through your goals and reorganize them in such a way that you are comfortable with. Take a walk and live your phone behind so that you are not distracted while you relax and get things in perspective.

When simplifying your life, think of the following questions to help you make things more workable and peaceful for you;

- What are the low priority and high priority activities?
- Is there a way I can feel at peace despite a very long to-do list?
- Are there things that are I need to say NO to so that I can improve my productivity?

Practical ways to simplify your life

Spend at least 10 minutes meditating

Meditation is one of the fastest ways in which you can simplify your life and improve your willpower. When you meditate, you are simply allowing your brain to focus and resist rumination. According to research, spending 2-3 days practicing 10 minutes of meditation improves your brain's focus, boosts energy, and lowers stress. There are so many meditation techniques that are available online, and you can practice them every morning you get up for a chance to seize the day.

Work on your posture

According to studies, posture plays a very critical role in

strengthening one's willpower. Each time you find yourself slouching, all you have to do is allow yourself to sit upright/straight. This simple technique makes your life easy by boosting your degree of perseverance.

To get started, allow yourself to correct your posture each time you find yourself slouching, whether at the workplace or home. Trust me; it takes so much willpower to sit up straight. Each time you sit up straight, you are doing an exercise of your willpower muscle. What better way to make your life easy and simplified?

Keep a food diary

The other way you can make your life simplified is keeping a food diary. Interestingly, most people do not log all the food they eat. However, when you do this, you are in effect, improving your willpower. Plus, this has the benefit of ensuring that you keep track of what you eat and that everything on your food diary is healthy and offers you all the nutrients you need for a healthy body and mind.

One of the Apps you can download to help you do this is the MyFitnessPal app. This is a simple food diary application with a large database of foods and their nutritional information. With just two weeks of a food diary, trust me; you will be better placed to resist temptations.

Use your opposite hand

Just as you did with your posture, try to use your left hand if you are right-handed or right hand if you are left-handed. The truth is, your brain is wired to use a certain hand dominantly. However, when you start using the other hand, you are simply engaging your brain to train itself to do what would otherwise be "impossible." The good thing is that as you practice using the opposite hand, you are improving your willpower.

To get started with this exercise, all you have to do is select sometime during the day when you can dedicate to using your left hand. It does not necessarily have to take over an hour to get results. From experience, more than an hour only tires you, and your willpower is drained. When you finally get around to using your hand, you will realize how easy it is and hence learn to see possibilities as far as your tasks and goals are concerned.

Correct your speech

You can also try to change your natural way of speech so that instead of saying "hi" or "hey," you say "hello." If you train your conscience to instinctively correct speech, the truth is that you are increasing your willpower to perform better and improve your productivity at work and home.

To get started, choose some part of the day when you can practice correcting your speech. You can choose the words that you would like to start with. For instance, you can start with trying not to use contractions such that instead of saying don't, you simply say do not! Just like the other exercises, when you do this for two weeks, your willpower and level of productivity will be vastly improved.

Create and then meet self-imposed deadlines

If you have been in college before, then it is familiar to you how last-minute studying for a test can be like. You have a few hours to cram for the test! At this point, what is happening is that your willpower is taxed with trying as much as possible to shut out all forms of distractions so that you can focus on studying.

Using the same principle, studies showed that when you create self-imposed timelines, you are simply challenging yourself to work better and respond better to timelines on serious projects, hence avoiding procrastination. It will allow your willpower if significantly strengthened.

To get started, select a task from your to-do list that you have been postponing for too long. Set a deadline for getting the task done and ensure that you adhere to it. If you keep doing this for at least two weeks, you will finally be able to clear your backlog, boost your self-discipline, and improve your productivity.

Keep track of your spending

Just as most of us do not track what we eat, so do our spending. When you start keeping track of how much you spend each day and on what items, you are training your mind and willpower to stick to things that matter most.

Simply start by downloading a budgeting app such as Mint to your mobile phone. The good thing with such an app as Mint is that it connects to your bank account. When you review your spending daily, this in effect increases your focus and ability to resist the temptation to spend on unnecessary things, and this will also translate to your level of productivity.

Be mindful of your automatic decisions

Most of the time, the reason why we keep putting off tasks is that we allow ourselves to get lost in thought that we do not think twice about what actions we take and they happen automatically. One thing that you need to train your brain is to take time to think about what actions to take and decisions to make to increase the ability to focus on what is important while resisting the urge to yield to temptations.

To get started, it is important that you try as much as possible to catch yourself in an automatic habit and then take a minute to reflect on why you are doing it. You may want to question why you take a certain route to work instead of the other, which is even shorter, why you take three sugars in your tea when one tastes just fine. You can think of other things that you typically do and start changing them. This has the impact of improving both your level of concentration and self-control.

That said one thing that you have to note is that all your body muscles play a role in what you are and how you perform tasks, whether at home or in the workplace. They contribute to your willpower, and with the right practice, you can use them to simplify your life. These exercises go a long way in helping you improve your level of concentration, perseverance, and self-control, all of which have a role to play in combating procrastination and improving your productivity.

Think of training your willpower as though you are training for a marathon. When you are starting, you may not be able to run all 26 miles or so. However, with practice, you can perfect your skills and complete the marathon. In the same way, we have discussed quite several ways that can help simplify your life, improve your willpower, and boost your productivity. The truth is, when you are just getting started, it is hard to move from procrastinating directly to not procrastinating. However, with the right practice, you can slowly train your brain to take on important tasks to completion with the accepted timelines.

One Last Word

Procrastination is indeed a very serious problem that impacts your life negatively in so many ways. Naturally, human beings have always been inclined to have the least amount of resistance to procrastination. Well, the truth is, each time we put off something we know that we should be doing, there is a voice inside telling us to stop procrastinating. What is unfortunate is that we silence that voice by telling it that we still have more time the next day to complete it, and before we know it, the deadline is just a few hours away.

Today, procrastination has a huge role to play in our lives; whether at the workplace or home. It can come from anywhere. What makes us procrastinate too much varies from one individual and situation to another. In most cases, we waste so much time on tasks that we think are "enjoyable" and put off those that we think are "boring" yet these are the most important and urgent of them all. Sometimes, we think that we should put off the tasks at hand until we have a better angle to solve them.

It is important to note that when we keep putting off tasks that we should be doing, we are increasing chances of anxiety and stress, and this eventually rubs off on our performance and level of productivity. In this book, we have discussed in depth the steps that you can take to overcome procrastination and the various actionable tips to help you start your day on fire.

Realize that, is no one that is perfect and so you will never be able to attain perfection even if you tried. Even the most successful people in the world are far from being perfect. However, the most important thing is for you to express your willingness to give yourself a chance to try and learn as you go. You have to step out of your comfort zone so that you can tap into your growth mindset. You will be surprised just how smart and equipped you are!

So, what are you still waiting for? Practice the exercises we have discussed in this book, and you will be on your way to kicking procrastination, embracing change, pursuing your goals, and attaining success and happiness in life.

Good luck!

Manufactured by Amazon.ca
Bolton, ON